W9-CNV-008

A Gift For:

From:

the gift of acceptance

janine shepherd

inspired LIVING

ALLEN&UNWIN

Hallmark

For my dad

Introduction

Acceptance is a lived experience. It can't be given to you—you need to earn it. Most often it comes from living through the most excruciatingly painful and difficult times. When it comes to acceptance, I thought there wasn't much else I needed to learn.

In 1986, I was a member of the Australian ski team and was in training for the 1988 Winter Olympics in Calgary. Having returned from Europe with an invitation to train with the Canadian team in the lead-up to the Games, I was on top of the world. This was everything I had worked for in my life and nothing was going to stop me from achieving my dream. I didn't just want to represent my country at the Olympic Games—every athlete's dream—I wanted to put Australia on the map as a force to be reckoned with; to show the world that we could be the best in the world at winter sports.

A split second is all it takes to change a life forever. While on a training bike ride with my fellow team-mates I was hit from behind by a speeding utility truck and left with extensive and life-threatening injuries: broken neck and back in six places, broken collarbone, five broken ribs, broken arm, broken bones in my feet, head injuries, internal injuries, massive blood loss.

I was airlifted from the scene of the accident to a large spinal unit in Sydney. By the time the helicopter arrived at the Prince Henry hospital, my blood pressure was forty over nothing. Any hope of survival was all but gone and my parents were called with the news that every parent dreads: that their child had been involved in a tragic accident and was not expected to live.

To this day, I still don't remember the accident. My last clear memory was riding up a hill with the sun shining in my face, then blackness. The doctors called it post-traumatic amnesia, but I know that the reason I don't remember is that at the point of impact I had already left my body. I drifted between two worlds, fighting the toughest battle of my life, trying to decide whether it was worth coming back to a body that was so badly broken.

Once my neck and back were stabilized, it was the blood loss that was the major concern. The internal bleeding was critical and for over a week they fought to keep me alive. I continued to bleed as fast as they could pump the blood into me and at one point they called my parents outside to tell them to prepare for the worst: there was nothing else they could do. My family and friends maintained a vigil at the hospital, hoping and praying that I would make it.

When I finally regained consciousness, I really didn't have an understanding of what had happened to me. The experience was surreal, dreamlike. One minute I was an elite athlete on my way to the Olympics and the next I was lying paralyzed in a spinal ward.

The doctors informed us that although the neck break was stable, the vertebrae in my back were completely crushed. The only hope of walking again was to undergo delicate spinal surgery. They would remove my broken ribs to fuse my back together. Without the surgery, I would be in a wheelchair for the rest of my life.

Although the surgery was deemed a success—they had removed as much of the bone that had lodged in my spinal cord as they could—the damage, they said, was permanent. It was the central nervous system and there was no cure. If I walked again it would be with calipers and a walking frame. I would have little feeling from the waist down and would need to use a catheter for the rest of my life.

"You are what we call a partial paraplegic," the doctor informed me, "and you will have to rethink everything you do in your life because you will never be able to do the things you did before."

As I absorbed her words, struggling to make sense of what she was saying, I tried to picture what my life would look like now. If I couldn't ski again—or run or play sports—what would I do with my life? I was an athlete and now I faced a life of permanent disability. Why has this happened? I asked, and why me? If there was a reason, what could it possibly be? What good could possibly come out of this?

After almost six months in the spinal ward, I returned to my home in a wheelchair and a plaster body cast to protect my back. My only thought was of learning to walk again and regaining some sense of purpose. Despite my best attempts at staying positive, I quickly slipped into a deep depression and, at times, I wished that I had not even survived my accident.

Ashamed of my body, I felt worthless. I went on an emotional roller-coaster between depression and anger. I struggled to keep up a brave face to everyone around me, while internally my life was falling apart. Everything I valued up to that day had been ripped from me and my self-image crushed. There were days that I didn't want to get out of bed and there were days that I just didn't.

Eventually, realizing that this accident was controlling every single moment in my life, I decided that if I was going to turn my life around I had to find something to replace everything I had lost. As much as I wanted to give up, I knew I couldn't . . . but why? Partly because I felt I owed something to my parents, and to myself, but also because I had a deeper understanding that there was something larger at work, and that gave me something to hope for and something to fight for.

In a sense, this was another hill and I was going to use the same technique in my recovery that I used when I ran or rode my bike up a hill—put my head down and just focus on the next step or the next pedal push until I was at the top.

Sometime later, and with that shift in attitude, I was sitting outside in my wheelchair when an airplane flew overhead.

"That's it," I thought, "if I can't walk, then I'll fly!"

The seed was planted and although it seemed completely ridiculous and far-fetched, I had nothing to lose. I called a flying school and enquired about a test flight, a TIF as they called it—a trial instructional flight.

Weeks later, Mom and another friend drove me out to Bankstown Airport and carried me into the flying school. I did not look like the ideal candidate to get a pilot's license! Still covered in a plaster body cast, I was lifted into the aircraft for the first flight.

Although I couldn't use my legs, I could use my arms. Once airborne, the instructor told me to take the controls and head towards the mountain in the distance. I took the controls and I was flying! I was a long, long way from the spinal ward. I knew right then that I was going to be a pilot. I didn't know how on earth I would ever pass a medical, but that didn't matter, because now I had a dream and nothing was going to stop me.

I planned, I focused, I was dedicated. I strove for excellence—whatever that meant for me. At one point it was just to use a catheter or maybe taking my first step or walking unaided. At first all I could do was to lie on the ground and lift my leg just a few inches—it took all my strength just to do that. It wasn't much but it was better than nothing. I couldn't look back; all I could do was to look forward.

While the doctors continued to put my body back together again, I lost count of how many operations I had and the setbacks I encountered along the way. At one point it seemed to be one step forward, two steps back—just when I would gain some ground, I would find myself back in the hospital with a complication or infection of some sort.

Coming to terms with my shattered Olympic dreams and refusing to believe what expert medical staff told me about my chances of recovery, I had to focus every sinew of my being on healing not only my broken body but also my crushed morale. Everything had shifted from my outer life to all my inner victories.

The accident had happened. I couldn't change that, but what I could change was the way I chose to see my future. With my personal mantra of loving the hills, I kept reminding myself that this was all part of something bigger and I was responsible for whatever the future held. My destiny was now a matter of choice, not chance.

I saw each hill, each challenge, as a lesson to teach me more about myself and my life purpose. This was the shift that enabled me to move forward and explore deeper aspects of myself than I had before. I realized that life, however imperfect, offered an opportunity to grow. I discovered strengths deep within that I never knew existed and built upon each challenge with the skills that I learned along the way.

Confounding doctors, and despite remaining a partial paraplegic, I did eventually learn to walk again. And I did learn to fly. I went on to gain my private pilot's license, my commercial pilot's license, my instructor rating and my aerobatic rating. I then went on to work as an aerobatics flying instructor, teaching people how to fly upside down!

And although there was always some doubt over whether I would ever be able to fall pregnant due to the extent of my internal injuries, I did eventually marry and have three beautiful children.

So much had changed and writing about my life in my autobiography *Never Tell Me Never* had launched an entirely new career on the public speaking circuit. Sharing my story with others, both through my writing and speaking, has been a great blessing for me and has given me the opportunity to heal on so many levels.

It was the seemingly intangible qualities—the mental attributes I had developed over my lifetime as an athlete—that gave me the resilience and fortitude to hang in there despite the overwhelming odds against me. Courage, determination, commitment, responsibility, self-sacrifice, perseverance and gratitude to name a few—these were my tools that I had used to rebuild my life.

Thinking that I had climbed the highest mountains and overcome the greatest obstacles that life could possibly throw at me, I believed there couldn't possibly be any battles that could leave me unstuck. I was wrong.

Up to this point, I had lived life with an understanding of what my body could and couldn't do. I had learned to manipulate my world through my body and, as important as this was at the time, I had no idea of how much more there was to the journey, how much deeper I needed to go and how much more there was for me to learn.

Indeed, over the years I have been asked many times how I managed to survive such horrendous injuries and find the inner strength to achieve all that I have in my life. And until recently, I would have struggled to answer this question adequately. I believed it was a combination of qualities that enabled me to not only survive but thrive after my accident.

However, I had overlooked a crucial lesson—one that embodied the quality that I now believe to be the single most important one in our lives. This was revealed to me by someone I met in a small country town.

I had arrived at the Little Billabong hall as part of my tour called "Lifting the Spirit." I planned to travel to areas where those on and off the land had been struggling with drought, floods or any of the other travails that are a part of living in remote areas.

Mingling with the crowd, I began a conversation with an elderly lady. "It's wonderful that you have come out here," she remarked. "It is just what we needed."

I was taken by her spirit and frankness. She was what the bush was about—real, down-to-earth people. I loved speaking and sharing with all of them and although I was the one presenting my story, it was their stories that gave so much back to me.

She began to recount her life to me, which I found fascinating.

"I have seven children," she told me matter-of-factly. "But I recently lost a son."

"I am so sorry to hear that," I replied.

"Oh no dear, don't feel sorry for me," she said. "Just like you, I've been given the gift of acceptance. No matter what happens in life, you've just got to get on with it."

Standing there, lost for words, I took in what she had said. The clarity that I had searched for for so long was staring me in the face. Acceptance was the quality that came before everything else and it had enabled me to move forward and find a new direction in life.

I knew I couldn't change what had happened, but I could change the way I saw my life from that point on. Allowing, not resisting, accepting what had happened to me had opened the door to possibilities that I had never before considered. It brought positive change, healing and growth. It had given me my life back . . . and more.

Acceptance is the one quality I am constantly reminded of when life throws me more challenges or more hills to climb.

The past few years have been equally challenging in terms of the "hills" I have encountered in my life. I have been through a marriage break-up, becoming a single parent to three children while trying to juggle the demands of work, many more operations and other physical setbacks on top of the challenge of living with chronic pain and permanent disability.

And then, as I sat down to write a book on acceptance, my life was turned upside down once again. The relationship that I had been in for almost two years, that I had put my heart and soul into, ended abruptly. This rocked me to my core and challenged everything I thought I knew about the subject. It was as if the universe tapped me on the shoulder and asked, "Okay, how much do you really know about acceptance?" Not as much as I thought, and it forced me onto a whole new level of healing and self-understanding that I had not experienced before.

Although I had a new life-affirming perspective, the truth was that much of what I had achieved was done with a combination of hard work, force and struggle. However, this was never going to sustain me in the long term and it was now time to learn the art of surrendering to the stillness and allowing a deeper level of self-love, peace and acceptance to enter my life.

Now I find myself in a place where acceptance has taken on an entirely new meaning. It is now no longer all about accepting only the circumstances of life, but about accepting all of the parts of myself that I left behind while I was busy getting on with my life.

Yes, I had healed my body on a certain level, but I had not really healed the deepest parts of my soul and this was now a journey into my heart. There were so many parts of myself that I had not embraced, accepted or learned to love and it was now time to enter into a relationship with all of those forgotten and ignored parts and heal them.

It was no longer about trying to be strong all the time, but giving myself permission to feel the whole range of emotions, which I had previously, and perhaps unwittingly, taken as a sign of weakness. I now see that when I allow myself to feel it all, that is when I am at my most courageous. I am gentler with myself and being vulnerable and authentic has become my priority.

Accepting all of life, the joyful and the most painful, has given me not only a new way of *doing* but also of *being*. I now see acceptance is a process, there are many layers and it is all about timing. There are times when I struggle to accept and that's okay, too.

Paradoxically, I can now accept the times of non-acceptance when I feel stuck and unable to move forward and I feel comfortable with that. I now know that when I am in that space, it is only because there is healing trying to happen. I have learned to let go and let God in and realize that I don't need all the answers now; I know they will come with time.

A willingness to see things as they are, understanding the ephemeral nature of life, is the greatest gift we can give ourselves. When we accept life as it is, we make peace with life and we stop expecting that it should be anything other than what we have been given.

My gift is to share some more intimate parts of this journey with you.

With love,
Janine

Sometimes I forget these lessons myself and need reminding,
but that doesn't mean I am a failure . . . just human.

So . . .

In accepting . . .

I see that even if I don't have the answers yet,
I can still love the questions.

In accepting . . .

I give up believing other people can make me happy.
I am a gift to myself, my own best friend.

In accepting . . .

I see that life is not about *having* it all,
but *loving* it all.

In accepting . . .

I find it easier to slow down and stop *doing*,
and instead I relish the moments
of pure *being*.

In accepting . . .

I realize that we are all the same,
yet uniquely different.

In accepting . . .

I see that a simple act of forgiveness
is an opening to divine grace.

In accepting . . .

I begin each morning with gratitude, thinking
of five things to give thanks for.

In accepting . . .

I quit being dependent on other people's opinions.
How I feel about myself has become
more important.

In accepting . . .

I begin to see that meeting my own needs does not make
me selfish and that when I meet my own needs I am
more able to meet the needs of others.

In accepting . . .

I can tell that getting older has nothing to do with age
and everything to do with attitude.

In accepting . . .

I begin to laugh at the things that brought me so much
pain in the past. I know that not being able to
laugh at life clouds the experience.

In accepting . . .

I surrender to life as a process that
is forever unfolding.

In accepting . . .

I am aware that when I struggle to understand
another person, it is never about them
and always about me.

In accepting . . .

I understand that there are no problems in life,
only lessons.

In accepting . . .

I quit carrying around the past or anticipating the future
and live fully in the present moment, recognizing
that *now* is the only time I will ever have.

In accepting . . .

I see that healing is about loving myself and when
I love myself, I love the whole world.

In accepting . . .

I recognize my purpose and, in doing so, am able to use
my unique gifts to best serve others.

In accepting . . .

I see that life is one huge personal development course
and I am still a long way from graduating.

In accepting . . .

I feel comfortable saying "no"
instead of "yes."

In accepting . . .

I welcome the sorrows as well as the joys.
I see them as polarities of a
balanced life.

In accepting . . .

I see that I have a story, but I am
not defined by my story.

In accepting . . .

I see that life is not about collecting *things*,
it is about collecting *experiences*.

In accepting . . .

I can speak from my heart and know that
not hurting myself is just as important
as not hurting another person.

In accepting . . .

I see that abundance is less about money
and more about state of mind.

In accepting . . .

I know that the moment you let go of inner
resistance to pain and suffering, you
open a window to the divine.

In accepting . . .

I see that every problem has a lifespan.

In accepting . . .

I welcome miracles.

In accepting . . .

I understand that forgiving myself is just
as important as forgiving others.

In accepting . . .

I see there are no accidents,
only experiences.

In accepting . . .

I react less and respond more.

In accepting . . .

I realize my choices come from a place of
awareness and I take responsibility
for where they take me.

In accepting . . .

I understand that loving the hills, or challenges
in life, is about cultivating the
virtues of the heart.

In accepting . . .

I listen to my heart instead of my head,
trusting it will always lead me
to the highest good.

In accepting . . .

I trust in the great mystery of life. I don't have
to understand everything—I enjoy watching
it unfold, knowing that the purpose will
eventually reveal itself.

In accepting . . .

I begin to love my time alone and look
forward to getting to know
myself even better.

In accepting . . .

I realize that even though life is simple,
it is not easy. And that's okay.

In accepting . . .

I know that life is filled with hills, with tough times,
but when you learn to love them they are
not tough anymore.

In accepting . . .

I see that following my truth will bring healing;
not following it will bring pain.

In accepting . . .

I simplify my life. This is an ongoing process
that lightens my load.

In accepting . . .

I see that focusing on physical pain only
adds an emotional element to it.

In accepting . . .

I experience the joy in helping others.
When I do, everything I desire
flows naturally to me.

In accepting . . .

I come face to face with my deepest fears and
confront them. I realize they were never as
bad as I had imagined, and they show
me how courageous I can be.

In accepting . . .

I no longer judge others—everybody is doing their best with where they are, at any given time (including me).

In accepting . . .

I know that the only actions I will be
truly rewarded for are my own.

In accepting . . .

I recognize that when I argue about something
I need to remind myself, "Do you want to be
right or do you want to be happy?"

In accepting . . .

Embracing the *is*-ness of every situation is the
only way to find clarity and move forward.

In accepting . . .

I ask myself constantly, "What is the gift in this?"

In accepting . . .

I see that healing comes not through running
from the pain, but living through
the experience.

In accepting . . .

I decide that every obstacle is an opportunity
to take on an even greater challenge.

In accepting . . .

I take responsibility for my life and don't
expect anyone to fix things for me.

In accepting . . .

I see that we all have a spark of divinity within us—
we are all connected by a common thread.

In accepting . . .

I begin to understand that although life might
not seem perfect right now, the present
circumstances are perfect.

In accepting . . .

I no longer resist or fight reality;
nor am I resigned to it.

In accepting . . .

I see that acceptance precedes expansion
and awareness precedes change.

In accepting . . .

I write to understand, not to be understood.

In accepting . . .

I see that it is not the meaning *of* life that is important, but the meaning *in* life.

In accepting . . .

I see that death, as we know it, is just an illusion.
We don't *go* anywhere. We are already here,
there and everywhere.

In accepting . . .

I understand that my responsibility is not
to change the world, but to change
the way I experience it.

In accepting . . .

I see the strength in others and this helps
me see the strength in myself.

In accepting . . .

I know my thoughts are energy. Before I give
that energy away, I think about how I want
to expend it and with whom.

In accepting . . .

I know it's not *what* I do but *how* I do it
that is important.

In accepting . . .

I recognize that my best ideas come when I have
nothing to lose. Tough times inspire creativity
and open the door to infinite possibilities.

In accepting . . .

I see life as an adventure.

In accepting . . .

I have stopped trying to *fix* other people.
That is their responsibility.

In accepting . . .

I can sit in silence and slip into the gap. I can hear
the universe whispering in my ear and know
I am never alone.

In accepting . . .

I see that perspective is everything.

In accepting . . .

I see that every day I have the opportunity to make
choices that will redefine the rest of my life.

In accepting . . .

I see that the more grateful I am in life,
the more life gives me to be
grateful for.

In accepting . . .

I know that my spirit is unstoppable.

In accepting . . .

I realize that we all express our divinity in our own
unique way. There is one path, but many ways.

In accepting . . .

I see that even when I feel like I have lost it all,
that loss was necessary to make room for
the life that awaits me.

In accepting . . .

I give myself permission to feel it all. I can sit
with every emotion knowing that even my
tears have a purpose and they are just as
important as the moments of laughter.

In accepting . . .

I understand that I no longer have to struggle for
the answers. In perfect time, the solutions to
my problems arise from the quiet place
in my heart.

In accepting . . .

I end each day with gratitude, thinking
of all the things to give thanks for.

In accepting . . .

I know that inside me there is a place of security,
stillness and peace—the heart and mind of God
with which I am forever connected.

In accepting . . .

I stop asking, 'Why me?' and instead
begin to ask, 'Why not me?'

In accepting . . .

I reflect on the questions . . .

Who am I?

What is my purpose in life?

Where am I going?

. . . and I am still doing it.

With love and gratitude

To Nano, whose words of wisdom gave life to this book.

To my publisher Jane Palfreyman, who had the vision and passion to share this journey with me from the beginning.

To my editor Vanessa Pellatt, whose patience and editorial skills have helped connect the reader to each page.

To Brett Lamond for seeing the big picture. Your advice and support have enabled me to stay focused and on purpose.

To Marianne Pagmar, my soul mate on the other side of the world. Your love and laughter are a blessing.

To Toni Murray, a gifted teacher whose wisdom and insight have guided me over the years.

To Sarah and Darren Powell, who have worked beside me and supported me in my creative and personal life. Love you guys.

To Ange Clarke, my paddling partner. The times spent drifting along the river with you always feeds my soul.

To my spiritual family Ofra, Dominique and Bhakti-Das. Your love and daily conversations keep me connected to my heart at all times.

To Lucy Palmer, whose gift for words inspires me. You challenge me, you make me laugh and you listen. Your friendship and support are invaluable.

To my beloved family Max, Shirley, Kim, Kelley, Morgan and Hap. The best support crew anyone could ever hope for.

And, as always, to my three beautiful children Annabel, Charlotte and Angus, whose unending love makes everything possible.

If you have enjoyed this book
or it has touched your life in some way,
we would love to hear from you.

Please send your comments to:
Hallmark Book Feedback
P.O. Box 419034
Mail Drop 215
Kansas City, MO 64141

Or e-mail us at:
booknotes@hallmark.com